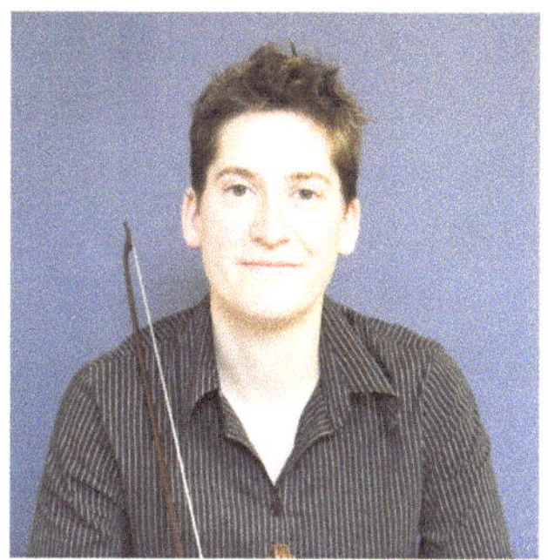

Violinist **Rachel Harris** has been a member of the English chamber music ensemble The Brook Street Band since 1997 and is the leader and director of Ensemble Schirokko Hamburg, which she formed in 2007. She has produced numerous CDs to critical acclaim with both ensembles.

As well as teaching privately, she is frequently invited to coach both baroque and modern orchestras. She is a guest coach and lecturer at the Hochschule für Musik und Theater Hamburg.

This book is dedicated to my friends and colleagues, with whom I have had the pleasure of many years (decades!) of wonderful music-making, as well as countless informative conversations. In spite of the present difficulties, I look forward to many gigs and projects with you in the future!

This book has been over nine years in the making and does not claim to follow historical sources. It is more the result of decades of joy, frustration and observation in the world of freelancing.

I would like to thank my sister Jennifer Harris for her invaluable advice on the wind section and for her help with the proof-reading. It was an enthusiastic Emily White who gave the text a final polish, many thanks indeed! I am also especially grateful to Christoph Harer for his willingness to give continuo cellists a voice. And a huge thanks to all those who have supported me with their enthusiasm for seeing this finally get published: it couldn't have happened without you!

Hamburg, December 2020

Rachel Harris

Rachel Harris

ORCHESTRAL TECHNIQUE
in action

Guidelines for playing

in a historically informed orchestra

aimed at student string players

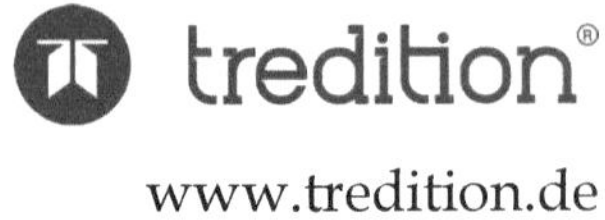
www.tredition.de

ORCHESTRAL TECHNIQUE in action
© 2020 Rachel Harris
© photo Rachel Harris: Valérie Wagner

Verlag und Druck: tredition GmbH, Halenreie 40-44,
22359 Hamburg

ISBN
Paperback: 978-3-347-04494-4
Hardcover: 978-3-347-04495-1
e-Book: 978-3-347-04496-8

Printed in Germany

Bibliografische Information der Deutschen Nationalbibliothek:
Die Deutsche Nationalbibliothek verzeichnet diese Publikation in der Deutschen Nationalbibliografie; detaillierte bibliografische Daten sind im Internet über http://dnb.d-nb.de abrufbar.

Contents

Introduction

Setting out to become a professional musician generally leads to a career within an orchestra. And we usually prepare for this by ensemble practise and playing lots of orchestral music, mostly in 'modern' orchestras. Tutors are often there to guide the sections during rehearsals, repertoire is expanded and concert experience gathered. However, I feel that a practical guide seems to be missing as to how we can best survive in the tough world of freelance orchestral playing. As this is a field of many areas, these guidelines concentrate on the necessities of freelance string players, especially within the world of historically informed performance practise. It might, of course, be of interest to other orchestral performers.

Although I have attempted to gather some of the things necessary for playing well in an orchestra, this book does not pretend to be comprehensive, or answer all questions encountered during rehearsals or concerts. I have used both the terms 'leader' and 'concert master' as they are interchangeable.

1 PREPARING FOR A PROJECT

It is one thing to practise at home, another to play an exposed part in a group! There is nothing comparative to rehearsing as a section, however here are some suggestions how to prepare:

- Make absolutely certain that exposed bars are perfect – e.g. use 'safe' fingering. When playing in a group it is very hard to hear yourself, so tactile knowledge then becomes so much more important.

- Playing in a group IS more stressful than at home! Try practising with the metronome (yes, a VERY good aid!) many notches higher to simulate the added adrenaline.

- It is sometimes harder to read the music because of having to share a stand so that the music is no longer directly facing us. Read the music from an angle to get used to the new picture.

- Fingerings in the part might help ... until the copies are replaced by real music where there is nothing written in... Memorise the fingerings! Try not to write anything in the part, but memorise as much as possible. This also gives more flexibility when rotating.

- Search out the difficult bits (with Bach it is very often a middle section in a horrible key!) and give them extra attention.

- Listening to recordings is one of the best ways of getting to know a piece!

- Playing along to a recording (especially on headphones) is a great simulation of how it might work in a group where you hear more of others and less of yourself.

- Get hold of a score.

- Know what the choir or soloists are singing. Know how their words and need to take breaths affects the line you are playing (especially if you are playing the same line).

- Trying to visualise the situation and the rehearsal room, church or concert hall as much as is possible is a great asset in reducing nerves. Especially helpful before a concert.

Leaving early enough to get to the rehearsal on time always makes a good impression and means you are not stressed from travelling. You can even have a nice chat before it all starts (all part of our work!). Rather a bit too early than arriving just in time, especially on Fridays because of heavier weekend traffic.

2 HOW AN ORCHESTRA MIGHT WORK

2.1 Hierarchy

To allow a rehearsal to flow well and to keep everyone happy (especially those up front!) it is helpful to understand the hierarchy of an orchestra. This is different for the winds and strings, as the functions of the groups are in themselves different.

Wind players work individually and yet have to create a unified sound. In the classical build-up of a wind section the seconds play with the firsts, and the firsts try to play equally together. The best set-up is one that easily allows this. That is why winds always want to sit in two rows, the firsts grouped in the middle. It can be that the first oboe takes the reins when something has to be said, but that is more down to what type of person they are. Seconds are very important within the ensemble, often doubling other firsts, e.g. second clarinet with first bassoon, and to create a homogeneous sound they have to be able to gauge how much input they should give. Wind parts doubling the strings (especially oboe and flute) are particularly tricky, because of the tuning. A bad set-up (i.e. no platform) between the winds and strings can make this much more difficult. For baroque music there is less of the hierarchy, it is much more individual and depends on the piece played, especially in early baroque. Winds need to be able to blend with the tutti sound of the strings when playing their line, such as the oboe d'amore in No. 3 of Bach's Christmas Oratorio, or the bassoon in the bass line generally. Here in particular the cellist leading the bass section must be careful not to 'go it alone' but to take the double bass/violone and the bassoon with them.

Strings on the other hand, have to find a way of playing one line in a joint way and yet form as a group with a varying number of voices, and, as this guideline is mainly for strings, I will go into that in more depth.

- Tutti players should refer questions to their section leader (but quietly, so as not to disturb the flow of the rehearsal)

- The section leaders should refer to the concert master

- The concert master refers to the conductor

This is especially in the case of bowings, when frequently whatever it was is solved before even reaching the conductor. If the concert master or the conductor is asked every little thing then not only does it drastically slow down the rehearsal, it could also raise the stress-levels of those at the front.

Questions should be asked quietly, or notes made to be asked in the break.

This ranking system also works backwards:

- When having stopped to make corrections, the first person to say something is the conductor

- Then the concert master

- Then the section leaders

It is of course always possible for a question (hopefully an intelligent one!) to be asked from the back. I suggest, however, that this rather strict advice is followed as closely as possible when the acoustics are difficult. When a room is over-acoustic and loud (very tiring for the ears and concentration!) or when it is a large group, players at the back find it difficult to hear and thus hard to take part in the rehearsal. Those having difficulties, such as the string players in the back desks, woodwind and brass sections will find it harder to concentrate and might switch off, to the disappointment of those seated at the front.

Note: a calm and friendly face seated next to the concert master is greatly appreciated by those further away!

2.2 A word on rotation

Rotating players in a group can be split up in to two parts: rotating within a project or (in a group which meets frequently in the same constellation) rotating from gig to gig but staying fixed during the whole project.

Project rotation, especially in a large group or a longer project, say, an opera production, gives almost all (the section leaders do not change position) the opportunity in getting to know the piece or pieces from many different angles. It also gives those at the back more of a chance to take part in the rehearsal and have a rest from the hard work of added concentration needed at the back. It is ideal for longer projects where rotation can bring an added sparkle in the group. It is not very good for shorter projects, where quick gelling is needed.

Gig rotation (rotating from gig to gig, but being fixed for the project) is an important means of keeping up enthusiasm, especially in the violin sections. If one player were to constantly be put in the tutti of the seconds, this person would after a while become unhappy with the situation, lose concentration, lack energy, become insecure and would give less input. If this person is sometimes given the first part, or the job of leading the seconds, then they can quickly become reanimated and more sure of themselves. It is a good way of showing all the players how much they are appreciated!

2.3 Body language

Body language can be a very useful tool when playing, especially when the person is conscious of their movements and knows how to use them. Section leaders can use carefully placed movements for a variety of things such as dynamics and the direction of a passage or rhythm.

Excessive movement is especially unwanted in the tutti strings, where attention is drawn away from the concert master or even the conductor. A concert master also needs to take care not to move (much) more than the conductor, as it reduces the authority up front, unless something drastically goes wrong and someone else needs to take the reins.

Knowing how to move calls for an awareness of your own habits. These habits (e.g. an automatic, habitual downward movement on every even beat) can impede musical expression and make life very difficult for fellow players. Attempting to play and at the same time execute movements meaningful to the musical line is a good exercise to help with awareness.

A short dictionary of movement for section leaders (multiple interpretations are possible):

- Eye contact – I need you to follow me, play together with me

- Eye contact, smiling – I'm enjoying our music making!

- Sudden movement – Attention! Look at me! Something new is about to happen!

- Turning to section – Are you with me? Or 'focus'!

- (When standing) in crouching position – piano, also possible while seated.

- (When standing) very upright – forte, also possible while seated.

- Sharp movements – precise playing, also hard sound.

- Round movements – more lyrical, mellower sound.

There is no end to the amount of variations of how to move, this is after all how we make music.

On a less musical note: sitting with crossed legs or leaning back while playing not only makes it harder to play but sends out a signal of disinterest or boredom which is possibly not intended. Feet placed firmly on the ground and sitting upright show alertness.

2.4 Personal input versus following placidly

The tutti-player's dilemma is made up of a constant searching for the right balance of personal input and following the section leader, concert master and conductor. The former involves more initiative and spontaneity, but if there is too much, then ensemble playing might suffer. The latter is helpful in playing absolutely unified, although at the cost of spontaneous musicality, which necessarily has to take a back seat. There is no perfect, inflexible rule for this, so it means having to be alert to what is called for in any given moment.

2.5 Following the conductor

There are a great many different ways of showing a beat, especially in the freelance world of non-specifically trained conductors. Often we have organists who, in their job as cantor, have to be extremely versatile: play the organ, organise the music, get the players, direct an amateur choir and professional musicians, and even find the funding for the project.

Generally, the conducting technique of instrumentalists taking up the baton can be anything between wonderfully clear and abysmally misleading, where we have to do our utmost to find where the beat is! They are not always aware of what they might be doing wrong (neither might we be), and are not always grateful for advice.

A beat is shown by a quick speeding up of the arm within a movement, be it in a downward or an upward direction. When directing a choir, this centre of movement is often at the top of the beat, whereas with an orchestra it is usually at the bottom. Sometimes, if the music calls for it, there is almost no centre to the beat (the beat looks more like a circle). In contrast to modern orchestras which often play purposefully behind the beat, historically informed ones seek to play on the beat.

At times, conductors will find it necessary to conduct 'before' the beat, often in order to get the choir to sing faster. In rehearsal it is then necessary to follow the conductor, to get the choir to realise what is happening, although this should be less strict in concert. Conducting 'before' the beat is also sometimes the case in operas, where a conductor might try to get the singer on stage not to drag while the orchestra follows the singer, not the conductor. Each conductor has their own way of dealing with these situations, some more extreme than others, and it means keeping a cool head, a good overview of the situation and knowing what the conductor wants!

2.6 Concert master/continuo cello advice

Only those feeling integrated and accepted can let themselves be led! Bringing in those at the back (be it strings or winds) with friendly glances can work wonders for getting a group sound. A job description for a leader/continuo cellist might be as follows:

- Can follow what the conductor is showing, conveying security if the conductor, say, does not show an entry.

- Can keep the focus of the ensemble even when the conductor is busy with another group (e.g. a choir).

- Can show the timing, articulation and musicality through their body language (the shoulders and back can be very informative!).

- Does not mess about (otherwise discipline will flag).

- Puts bowings in all the parts BEFORE the project starts. I like to do the upper strings and leave the bass group to themselves, fugal entries being an exception.

- Can create a joint sound: every orchestra sounds like the leader plays!

- Can help other musicians play their best!

- Leader: does not forget that the continuo is an equal leader. In early baroque only the bassus generalis leads, i.e. the chordal bass instruments. All other instruments are additions.

The concert master/cellist is a diplomat, recognising the authority of the conductor and mediating between the sections. If the atmosphere becomes tense then they can release it with a positive comment. Comments and suggestions should be formulated in a friendly yet firm manner, musical ideas first run by the conductor. It helps the whole project if the conductor (even if not good) has the feeling of being acknowledged and taken seriously – it is, after all, their project and their interpretation of whatever is on the programme.

Wishing the performers a 'nice concert' or a 'pleasant journey' just before going to play on stage makes the group even tighter and creates goodwill, just as thanking each person after the concert has taken place nicely rounds off the joint musical experience.

And finally, the concert master is the representative of the orchestra. If there are serious problems, or even just the rehearsal running over into the break, it is important for the climate that the leader points this out and makes sensible suggestions. Alternatively they can appoint someone capable to take over the job. Running over by only five minutes is not so bad, and most people are interested in finishing something already started rather than cutting it off. Things become more critical, though, if it looks like running over by more than 10 minutes. One possibility is to take the agreed time for a break but starting later, however this very often does not work with the schedule. I suggest therefore to keep an eye on the clock and recognise well in advance how the situation might turn out.

2.7 Rehearsal flow

A good rehearsal flow is not only the result of orchestral discipline. It is also dependant on how the rehearsal is taken. This might sound obvious, but is actually quite hard to spot. Concentrating too much on the technical side of things will bog down and slow the tempo, while focusing on interpreting the music has a high tempo and is eventually more accurate.

An example: the second violins have mezzo forte written in their part, but the conductor asks them to play a bit more. The cellos have a dotted rhythm which is slightly too dotted, they are to play it as written. The first violins need to soften their repeated quavers, as they are too hard. This is what I call rehearsing the digital way, as it assumes we all have the same (or similar) positions on our internal dials and no emotions. It is a detached, head-based way of rehearsing. We of course try to play as asked, but wonder why it just keeps on getting harder. Any technical adjustment without a musical, aka emotional foundation will not work and leads to insecurity. How are we to make good music without security or emotion?

However, if instead the conductor says to the seconds that we really need their scrunchy harmony just at that bit, or the cellos need to give a rich, sober impression with their dotted rhythms, or that the quavers in the first violins are gentle and stroking, we will find the musical reasons and our emotions connecting. Music-making will be vibrant and ever-renewing. It will also be incredibly easy to play together!

It is often not the fault of the conductor or director when a digital approach is taken. Players themselves fall into these traps, saying for example, that a particular rhythmical element is rushing, 'we need to *not* rush'. This is a digital accusation. The cause of this could be a number of things: maybe lack of aural/visual information (impossible to hear/see the pulse), maybe a lack of communication. It could also be due to different musical expressions at that point. Nobody rushes on purpose. Unfortunately, not only is digital rehearsing slow and draining, it often tends to be accusatory. The fastest and most exciting rehearsals have an explorative quality to them, getting to know the piece and finding out what is musically possible.

3 TUNING AND INTONATION

Tuning and intonation are sensitive subjects in most orchestras, and it helps to remember that no instrument or player is perfect, no matter how good they may be. Many factors influence this, be it the temperature, humidity, or even the time of day. Finding the right way of handling the different situations helps us feel securer and play better.

3.1 Tuning

Everyone needs to find the best way for them, but most essential is an accuracy achieved quickly, but without feeling hurried.

When the leader takes an A and passes it round, it is sometimes faster to tune one person at a time rather than the whole group, especially if it is small. Chords given by a keyboard instrument can also be good being more audible, but it allows for a wider interpretation of the pitches. An example can be found in historical tunings where the fifths for the strings are smaller than pure. If (for the A string) a D minor chord is given, then the tendency is naturally to try and find a pure fifth and make the A pure to the tonic, taking it too high in the end for the temperament. True accuracy therefore, can only come from a note given singly. Subsequent 'checking' to see if the strings are really right must be done with the knowledge of historical temperaments: if you have tuned ¼ comma mean-tone, then the fifths will NOT sound pure so there is no need to try and 'correct' them AFTER having tuned! If it is difficult to get used to the strings being other than pure, I suggest buying a tuning machine which has historical temperaments on it and practising your part with it at home. It can be very revealing!

In smaller ensembles sometimes every string is taken from the keyboard and passed on to each player, including the E string (although this is at the discretion of the concert master). The cellos and basses take the smaller fifths from the keyboard instrument, and viola players like to check their C strings with the cellos.

In slightly larger orchestras it can be more reliable to pass around an A and with each individual string instrument tuning pure fifths (but not larger!). The slight discrepancy of too large fifths (for historical temperaments) are less likely to be heard in the larger ensemble. The one downside of this is that the open G of the violins will in some cases be far too low, such as a fifth of a C major chord. In this case it helps to dampen the string with the finger just above the nut.

In even larger orchestras (classical and romantic) it may be better to do as in modern orchestras and take from the oboe, although my experience has been that it is still easiest for string players to take an A from a fellow string rather than a wind player. When it comes to tuning a chord, then the cellos and basses should keep as close to the keyboard instrument as possible, if there is one, the strings above taking care to temper their thirds and not making the fifths too small. It is helpful to know what part of the chord you are playing, e.g. the third, and what temperament is being used (and how it works!).

It is important to remember that tuning is a fundamental right, even if it breaks the flow of a concert. We need to sound good, otherwise we have no chance in showing our best side.

3.2 My personal tuning order

I have found it easiest to allow the cellist to take their notes from the keyboard first and tune the cello section, followed by the basses. I then take the A from them and check it with the keyboard.

My violin has quite a dark tone, so I personally have to take care not to be on the low side. Others with a brighter sounding instrument might have a tendency to take it higher, so it is important to know what sort of sound you produce.

I then pass it on to each group separately, playing strongly and as evenly as possible but taking care not to press the tone up when doing so (playing a string with more force raises the pitch slightly). When passing round the A it makes it easier for those taking it if the other sections are not tuning at the same time and not talking either. When giving or taking the A take care always to play in the same area of the string (not moving to and from the bridge) and match your bow stroke to that of the leader. This keeps the overtones even and similar to those of the leader, making it easier to tune. One thing that is also a great help is when the pegs move smoothly!

Once the strings all have their As, they finish by tuning the fifths.

3.3 Handling gut strings

With gut strings it is tempting to fine-tune the string by pressing the part of the string in the peg box to raise it or to pull the string to lower it. However, if the contact areas between the string and instrument, i.e. the nut and the bridge, have also been 'greased' to aid reliable tuning (I rub some dry soap into the groove) then pressing the string into the peg box will certainly not work. Even if it would hold for a short time, pressing the string only stretches it further, having the opposite effect of lowering the string. Pulling the string is more reliable, but as gut has tendencies rather like rubber, pulling very hard to lower it will not last long.

The fact that gut strings over time lose some of their tension should not lead to tuning higher than the A given, 'just in case', as it is far harder to correct tuning which is too high than one which is too low. Give the strings a bit of a tug to get them back to their optimal tension, then tune normally.

It is possible to have gut strings which are reliable: this means a lot of experimenting to find the right gauge for the instrument, as the wrong one will constantly change pitch. Interestingly, a good bowing technique is also advantageous in helping the strings stay in tune!

Old strings are also harder to tune as they lose their pure tone. Coming with played-in, fresh strings to a project gives you more confidence, and there are tricks for a student violinist's budget to keep the high costs of new strings at bay. One trick is to know that especially the upper strings only lose their purity in the area where they have been bowed. Turning the E or the A string round so that the bowed area ends up in the peg box allows for a pure string which is already partially played in!

On historical instruments, the projects can be at different pitches, depending on which period or geographical area is being performed. To get used to it, it is recommended to tune to the pitch some days in advance.

3.4 Winds

Winds also need their share of tuning, it is important as a string player not to forget this! They often feel neglected and rush in to tune while the strings are still busy (much to the annoyance of those sitting near them!). They need to be given the opportunity to tune separately, possibly needing notes other than an A. It is the concert master's job to find out which ones these may be, when they might be needed etc. and to remember this throughout the rehearsals and concerts. The winds also need to be able to have a moment to play their instruments freely (not hesitantly) to make sure all is in working order, it gives them confidence that the first notes of the session will work.

However, there are conditions when it is difficult for the winds to be at the agreed pitch, then the strings should adjust accordingly. In a cold room winds will possibly be lower and cannot come up enough, whereas in a concert the winds might rise because of the heat, there is nothing else for us to do but follow them. The main point being, that we should *listen* to the intonation and where it might be going: we are totally flexible and can accommodate easily!

The winds also tune to a different system than the strings, depending on how the section is built up. In a classical section, the more modern-influenced players there are, the more equally tempered the group may be. Mostly, however, the chords are tuned as pure as possible, although sometimes the instruments themselves can not tune any better and compromises have to be made. Even this does not always coincide with how the strings tune with their fingers. A wind section hears itself more clearly than the strings, which also contributes to the differences between the groups. It is also dependant on what types of instruments are used, classical ones or more inflexible romantic instruments. Baroque wind instruments are some of the most flexible in intonation and in that repertoire they can follow much more closely what the strings do, even sitting with the relevant voices.

3.5 Group intonation and sound

When getting together for the first time, it is better to find a group sound before correcting chords. A joint sound and conscious handling of the tone is essential for good intonation, as the overtones are then all in a similar range. Let me explain:

- a harsh and sharp sound produces many high overtones.

- the more overtones there are, the more accurate the intonation needs to be, as they all need to match each other.

- a darker, more mellow sound has fewer of the high overtones.

- the fewer overtones there are, the easier it is - for example playing a high passage in tune.

This means that if short, staccato playing is called for, it is helpful to concentrate on tone production and timing, as sharp (with many overtones) notes are not only harder to get absolutely together, but harder to tune.

If a passage in the strings is difficult to tune, then it helps first to check if open strings are in tune, change the fingering or even the bowing.

A standing chord which seems impossible to tune should be also be checked for balance, one basic rule being that the tonic should be strongest, the fifth somewhat weaker and followed finally by the third. If one part is doubling an octave higher, this should be somewhat quieter than the lower octave, otherwise it will be top heavy, the same goes for other chords, especially in parallel movement.

Intonation in a concert is more often than not completely different than in the rehearsal. There might be more humidity because of rain outside, nerves make strings go all over the place, it might also be suddenly much hotter than previously. Silent adjusting of strings helps, but can also be distracting and misleading to others. Beware of false corrections: as a natural phenomenon, the ear hears slightly higher notes as being more 'correct' than lower ones!

4 BALANCE

Balance is not only the result of how the groups are seated, but also of individual 'fitting in' with the group.

This might sound obvious: a string section will sound its most flattering when no single player audibly sticks out (that goes for the leader as well!). Most of the time we might be concentrating on other things (intonation, timing) than making a healthy, round group sound. Many of these issues can easily be solved by instead focussing on a homogeneous sound. Even though protected by the rest of the group, it is important neither to hide, nor to stick out. This calls for a good sense of judgement and knowledge of your own instrument. Keeping an overview of the balance helps with fitting in, although in moments of insecurity selective hiding is always accepted!

Here are some balancing tips:

- The larger the ensemble, the quieter piano has to be!

- In general, violinists (and even viola players!) should take care that their top string when open does not stick out causing an ugly bump in the dynamic level.

- The middle voices, i.e. the second violins and violas, should almost always be stronger than the outer parts as they have the disadvantage of lower voices frequently on the weaker (A and D) strings and having to play through a wall of sound created by those seated nearer the audience.

- The part on top (usually first violin) should not be too over-celebratory of the stratosphere but allow the other parts also to be heard.

- A rich and strong continuo sound will allow all the parts above them to 'rest' the harmony on their foundation.

4.1 Who wins?

It is quite possible to assume that those with the most authority are able to steer the orchestra with most ease. In practice, however, it is very different. If contact to those up front is lost, then a different hierarchy appears, one created by balance. First it is the lowest voice which is most powerful (bass section), then the loudest (trumpets, timpani). Trombones also carry a lot of this hidden authority. Therefore it is most important that these sections *in particular* follow the conductor or leader.

4.2 Seating

Seating also has an influence on balance – e.g. when the second violins or violas are seated opposite the firsts (to the right of the conductor) they will have to play louder than normal, with more articulation (this is what is lost most when playing away from the audience). Whoever is seated nearest the audience will form a barrier of sound over which the strings seated further in will have to play through. This goes for the winds as well, if they are unfortunate not to have platform. On a platform they can play over the strings; without one, it might be an idea to embed them, so to speak, in the hollow of the string group at the front (works best in a baroque formation), if that doesn't make them feel uncomfortable.

Another nice position is having the upper strings all on one side and the winds all on the other, with the continuo centre-stage.

In contrast to a true baroque positioning where the strings stand or sit in a line next to/opposite each other, I find it is easiest to make a warm group sound-cloud when seated in the 'bunch of grapes' formation (desks). It is helpful for the single players at the back of the firsts and seconds if they sit next to or near each other, then they have some form of contact and communication.

In the case of a tight baroque set-up of 3 x vl 1, 3 x vl 2 and 2 x violas it can be quite nice to have the violas between the two single violins at the back, although most of the time they prefer to be in the front line. For all those first violinists sitting in the very back, outside corner on their own: it really is one of the most difficult positions as there is hardly any amount of aural or visual information. Be brave and think of it as steering the group from behind!

Where to put the keyboard is a difficult question: if they are seated centrally, this drives a wedge into the string group. If they are at the back they might find communication extremely difficult. This is partly due to the amount of aural/visual information they need (more than other groups, especially when accompanying vocal soloists), and partly because they might not be as used to sitting at the back as, say, wind players who have often grown up at the back of an orchestra.

The continuo group likes to be near the keyboard, as they need to match their intonation with the keyboard's. This includes the bassoon in its continuo function. A clear sight-line between the leader and continuo cello is also advantageous.

It helps to decide the seating and space problem in advance of a project, although there is no perfect solution. This is also the time to sort out any lighting that might be needed, as rehearsal stamina and the ratio of correct : incorrect notes are directly related to this!

5 FUNCTIONS OF THE SECTIONS

Between the high baroque and romantic periods the functions of the groups was fairly clear-cut. Here is a short and very general characterisation of the string sections:

- Violin I, a 'prima donna', able to sing beautifully, must always be conscious of the fact that the melody can only enfold its beauty through harmony. Is also able (at times) to accompany another voice which has melody. Supported in rhythmical passages by other parts.

- Violin II, chameleon, supports the upper voice in harmony, is often bestowed with melody, bass line and rhythmical drive. An inner part with a passion!

- Viola, more often a rhythmical and harmonic force than violin II, also given bass functions and bestowed with some of the most gorgeous middle lines, unfortunately also some of the most boring ones, too. Less stress in these seats, it is said that this group has the longest life-expectancy...

- Cello, or basso continuo, continuous bass, the work horse with a bass line and rhythmical function carrying the whole of the harmonic world on their shoulders. The engine driving the orchestra.

- Violone or double bass supports the bass line by giving depth to the cello part. Often not noticed but missed when not there, they are the strongest rhythmical and dynamical force, and can, if they are good, drive all parts above (even the cellos) without any one noticing!

In fugues, canons and other compositions written more contrapuntally, these characteristics are often given up in favour of strict part-writing giving everyone a more equal role.

Knowledge of the function is helpful, although when dealing with, e.g. fugues, it is helpful to always assume that someone else also has a moving part at the same time when we have movement (automatically making us play rhythmically). It also helps to assume that we have parts that match another voice or are answering one. This practice of 'assuming' others play a similar thing is essential for ensemble playing as it opens us up in advance to what the others might be/are doing without compromising our own parts.

6 TECHNICAL PROBLEMS

6.1 General difficulties

Certain problems and difficulties arise regularly, I have tried listing some of the things to look out for. Being constantly on the look-out for possible problems and having a personal bodily awareness can speed up rehearsals enormously. Here is a generalisation of tempo problems:

Ⓐ <u>Tendency to rush:</u>

short notes with a hard articulation
duplets
rising passages
high passages
loud passages
brighter colours

Ⓑ <u>Tendency to drag:</u>

broad, smoothly articulated notes
triplets
descending passages (although to a lesser extent than rising ones)
low passages
quiet passages
darker colours

The typicalities in Ⓐ also influence one another, rearranging the problems, in the case of dynamics, thus:

Ⓐ Too loud or unwanted crescendos when there are:

short notes with a hard articulation
duplets
faster tempi
rising passages
high passages
bright colours

In the case of Ⓑ:

Ⓑ Too soft or unwanted diminuendos when there are:

broad, smoothly articulated notes
triplets
slower tempi
descending passages (although to a lesser extent than rising ones)
low passages
darker colour

This goes for articulation, colour, pitch and direction, too.

Here are some other examples and causes in detail:

- Pizzicato is a treacherous thing – it seems so simple and is yet so difficult to get together. A passage of pizzicato is usually too quiet and tends to rush. The concert master should keep the bow firmly in the hand so that those behind (who cannot see the finger doing the plucking) can follow the moving bow. Think of single pizzicati as preparing for a really good jump!

- Rising passages also have a tendency to rush, exploding with energy and enthusiasm.

- Loud notes also tend to be on the fast side for the same reason, whereas

- Quiet notes tend to get slower, having less energy.

- Sequences sometimes get the first note lengthened, hindering a good rhythm.

- A rest is often on the long side. One example being a rest, e.g. a quaver, followed by three quaver notes and this formula repeated as an accompaniment. Often the rest is too long (it helps to think of the rests as active).

- It might sound obvious, but counting rests well helps to play the next entry with confidence. If need be, use your fingers! Mental notes of what other parts are doing in the meanwhile also helps. Monteverdi's Vespers is good practise for this.

- Unwanted slowing down at cadences. This can very easily be solved by putting the cadential stress or weight a beat or two sooner. On the other hand, if more *ritardando* is required, then move the stress towards the end of the cadence.

Size matters: the larger the ensemble and the hall, the more likely it is to drag. A large orchestra (like the combined weight of all the players) is heavier and harder to get rolling, as well as being harder to stop. A small chamber group performing in a front room will on the other hand be more likely to rush. It is all a question of being aware of the right amount of energy needed!

The dynamics of a rehearsal or (especially) a concert can mean that insecurity arises in the form of the fear of placing final notes (marginally different to the unwanted *ritardandi*). It helps to recognise this and to try not to let it grow, although usually it takes place unconsciously and is hard to be stopped. Just the same sort of insecurity can crop up (often in the continuo group) in passages of repeated notes which occasionally change, e.g. every half bar. Then every change takes just slightly too long... These insecurities arise from inattention, or not wanting to stick out by being too early, and can only be reduced by discipline and courage!

6.2 Technical problems for strings

One very good example of a very 'stringy' difficulty is the Agnus Dei at the end of Bach's B minor Mass. Everyone is tired by the time the Agnus comes after the long stretch of concentration and emotional input prior to it. It is one of the hardest pieces for the violins and it helps to be generous with yourself and not force things, be it tempo, intonation or musicality. One very specific problem comes right at the very end with the final note: all the open G strings, very probably out of tune. It helps to 'cover' the string with the first finger, dampening it as close to the nut as possible, reducing all the overtones. This even works when the string is too high!

One sign that things are becoming difficult can be a feeling of breathlessness, something I feel is common with the Agnus. One way of solving this is either to play it using longer slurs than written to reduce the number of speedy and thus too loud up-bows, or to concentrate on an absolutely even and slow bow stroke. And how does the leader play it? It also helps the group to know where exactly the retake is.

A more general string issue is the manner of bowing. Care should be taken that up-bows are not louder or faster than down-bows, especially in dotted passages where there is a fear of moving to the wrong part of the bow. In a long, dotted passage the right hand can quickly become tense so it helps to throw in a hooked bowing from time to time.

Another specific bow consideration is one of how much is used. It is often that the whole bow length is used (e.g. in accompanied recitatives) just because we might be on autopilot, concentrating on following the conductor and singer. This autopilot should be switched off (permanently), to allow for more immediate music making! Always be conscious of how much bow is or is not needed.

Staying with the accompaniment of singers: it is helpful to know that they put their consonants *before* the beat, and their vowels *on* the beat. Assuming that they might have an up-beat in recitatives is often a good way of following. If, however, you can not hear the singer, then this is usually because the orchestra is too loud and is drowning them out (this is not only the case in recitatives).

One habit amongst the strings is not to articulate the start of a note well enough, something which almost every other instrument has to do, be it tongued, plucked or struck. Without articulation, the sound develops later and so the strings often get accused of being behind. This also goes for the end of a note, which sometimes tails off uncontrolled. It can be a wonderful effect, but care should be taken that this be done consciously and unanimously.

7 PSYCHOLOGY

7.1 The team

One of the things which interests me most is the psychology of an orchestra, how it comes together at the start of a project, how long this might take. Or how it is possible to gauge how another section is feeling or if the concentration levels are low. It is sometimes hard to predict how an atmosphere will be: the start of a season (i.e. Christmas) is still fresh and enthusiastic, the end of a season tends to be tired. Stress leading up to a gig does not necessarily mean that the atmosphere will be tense, on the contrary, if the stress (e.g. problems with the recording of a concert and whether all the performers allow it) is worked out with the well-being and respect of all in mind, then it is very possible for positive rehearsals to follow. And, something almost self-evident but forgotten by many conductors or leaders: a positive working climate brings out the best in us all.

Some helpful points to keep in mind:

- Orchestral playing is team work – the goal is to bring out as much music as possible by playing the best we can. It is important to remember that we are all on the same side and should do our best to support each other to get the best result: this is our job!

- Respect and the feeling of being valued gives us security. We are then more able to take those risks which invigorate music when playing.

- Carrying responsibility induces us to give more, rather than taking a back seat.

One thing which is beneficial for a good climate is psychological and emotional stability. If this is lacking (it may be one player at the back or even the conductor) it can disturb the balance of the whole. I do not want to go into the depths of psychological interpretation (I leave that to the professionals), let it suffice to say that a stable and independent person has music making as a foremost goal. This sounds easy, but it includes:

- being able to see the whole picture. This already solves many problems of communication.

- having a positive attitude.

- wishing to bring out the best in others (rather than trying to compete or find errors).

- being open to different interpretations (rather than taking a different one as a personal affront).

There are however times when there is a bad or unfriendly atmosphere, or when an issue crops up, or someone has personal, private problems. Sometimes the only solution is to reconcile yourself to the problem and take a back seat, as bad moods can ruin a whole project. And having said that: a friendly and positive musician is much more likely to get asked back.

7.2 Difficult desk-partners

Unfortunately, there are situations where it has not been thought out whether desk-partners will suit one another, and sometimes this can not only be musically unsatisfying, but in worst cases turn into a form of mobbing. Mobbing is a term used to describe a variety of behaviours that amount to emotional abuse. The behaviour of a single person or even a group of people can be hostile, making life difficult in a concerted fashion. It may not be hard to survive unsatisfactory music-making (although not much fun), but mobbing can be extremely subtle and hard to recognise, making possibilities to fight against it limited. One scenario could be a first project with a group and being mobbed by a member of that ensemble – what should you say, and to whom?? An answer is so difficult to find, so much depending on the situation at the time. Mobbing takes away any self-confidence and makes playing (and surviving!) extremely difficult, though recognising what is going on is a start. If you are a victim of mobbing, please seek help, whether it is from a friend or colleague you can confide in or a professional. If you notice that someone is being subjected to mobbing, do not hesitate to speak up!

7.3 Handling (someone else's) nerves

Something also to be prepared for is if someone else is nervous – this could affect your playing and make you nervous, too. Being nervous is infectious, and if the 'infection' is not to spread, then you have to stay calm and alert, concentrating on your own playing and on whoever else is also staying cool!

If however you yourself get nervous (e.g. in a solo), then here are some techniques which I find helpful. Experiment and see what you can find that works best for you. If you become nervous, then consciously set your personal 'Plan B' into action.

- Slow, small, calm breathing through the nose from the bottom of the stomach. If breathing is high in the chest, then breathing in for 2 counts and out for 3 can gently bring you down. The opposite of the 'fight or flight' reaction!

- Submerging yourself into the musical language can actually be a great help!

- Being highly attentive to other parts OR

- Being highly introvert, depending on the situation.

- 'Floaty', light and somewhat faster bow stroke.

For example, one of my personal Plan B's is to end a final long note on an up-bow, as my wrist shake only comes on a down-bow. No one seems to notice anything...

7.4 Friendly sections

A possible result of misunderstandings or of not being open to the needs of the other groups can mean that we end up with strings battling winds, or vice versa. It is often that the winds get bored by the strings sorting out their bowings (hindering the flow of the rehearsal), or the strings complain that the winds are out of tune (often it is their own strings). It is at times like these that we all need to slow down, take a step back and remember that we are all on the same side. There is after all, only the one team.

8 STAMINA

A long day of rehearsing comes to an end and everyone is tired. The rehearsal atmosphere should not be forced – everyone makes more mistakes when tired, but we should try to keep the discipline up. If the conductor insists on making precise corrections late in the evening, then it is up to one of the leaders to politely give the reason as to why something might not be working so well (i.e. the late hour, bad lighting).

Curiously, one way of surviving long days is to put more energy and involvement into the music than trying to save energy. Energy, coupled with enthusiasm, is nourishment to itself, whereas trying not to use any just drains what is left in the battery. This is why so many conductors seem to be able to go on forever, forgetting to stop for breaks or even forgetting to eat.

When it comes to the general rehearsal, this is sometimes so intense that the first (or only) concert is not as good as the run-through. It is also often said that a bad general rehearsal makes a good concert, this could be due to the heightened amount of concentration and stress in the concert. What often really helps is plenty of sleep, especially before a second concert. Sleep also has a crucial part to play in the reduction of nerves!

9 MANNERS

9.1 Work climate

A code of manners is also essential for a good atmosphere. If someone makes a mistake in a solo, then looking around and shaking heads could make them even more insecure, possibly being the cause of more mistakes.

These tips help make a good climate:

- No looking around, shaking of heads, 'tutting' or raised eyebrows when mistakes made – just ignore it! Positive communication, however, is welcomed!
- No shuffling feet or moving of chairs with a scraping noise.
- No absent-minded plucking of strings.
- No talking, unless necessary for the rehearsal.
- No smartphones, please have them switched off.
- No reading (unless a longer break in the rehearsal, and even then keep the ears glued to when you might be asked to play!).
- No audible talking at the back.

It is common for brass and woodwind players seated at the back to have their phones on, which is not really a problem, as long as this does not disturb the rehearsal.

9.2 Manners on stage

When coming on stage be aware that as soon as you walk out you are in the spotlight. In the following passages I have described what is commonly done in concerts.

When the conductor comes out, all stand when (if) the applause starts, slightly turned to the audience. When the conductor has finished bowing and has turned towards the orchestra, then we sit again. Sometimes, when playing a Passion as part of the church year, the audience (the congregation) might not clap, in which case we do not rise unless asked to do so.

Sometimes, between movements, it is necessary to hold the tension by not moving, or to have the instrument up early so as not to disturb by any sudden movements. Turning pages quietly (even when having to turn quickly) is always a good thing.

After the interval when the conductor comes in, then remain seated until shown to stand. During the clapping there should be no talking but the audience should be acknowledged. If we all start talking on stage then the audience will get the feeling that we find their appreciation of us worthless.

A good bow is not too fast (count to two when down, or as one of my very close colleagues says: "Hello toes!"), does not get in the way of the neighbour and is clearly led by the conductor or director. Some directors remember to let all those with solos or the continuo group stand up extra, and though this is very much appreciated is unfortunately not always the case. After the conductor has bowed and turned away from the audience, then we can sit down. It is also possible to follow the leader for all this.

Sometimes, before concerts and during intervals, it is possible for the audience to hear you warming up, in which case, play quietly so as not to disturb the special atmosphere for the audience.

Getting on and off stage should be done swiftly if all are coming out together. At times, we might go out quite early as the winds like to get settled. This is not a problem as long as we go out in smaller groups and not as a whole orchestra.

10 WORKING WITH CHOIRS

Choirs and churches can be a freelance musician's most frequent employer! The choirs are mainly built up of amateurs who are interested in making music to the best of their abilities and for their own enjoyment. For us, this might just be yet another gig, but for the choir it is possibly their highlight of the year! Their standard of music-making may be different to ours, but they do try their best and love the music (at times more than we do). Sometimes it is difficult for us to combine this with the search for our own highest standards, but when we work with them we should try to see it from their point of view: they might have had a hard day at work and then trying to get those top notes is just not so easy on a Friday night... Turning round with a smile, especially when your part is in unison with theirs, not only raises their awareness of what is going on around them, but also suggests that what we and they are doing, we are doing together.

It is also often that we get put up for the night with someone from the choir: we should keep our professional face on to the extent that we are still 'on duty' and representatives of the whole orchestra.

11 SURVIVAL TIPS FOR COLD CHURCHES AND ACCLIMATISED CONCERT HALLS

It is hard to play well when fingers are stiff with cold and icicles hang from noses, so even if this chapter does not really fall into a particular category for orchestral technique it offers some suggestions as to how to cope best in these situations.

First of all it is helpful to know if a church or hall is going to be cold or draughty (air conditioning can be dreadful!). In the winter season it is probably best to assume it will be cold and it is the job of whoever is doing the organising to find this out and pass the information on. Once it is clear that it will be a cold gig, here are some preparations you can make to stay warm during the long dark hours:

- Good, warm clothing, lots of it. Wool is still one of the warmest materials around: woollen pullovers, woollen socks, or thermal underwear. Scarves are very useful, if not around necks then over legs.

- Warm shoes/boots with good soles for stone floors. Battery-heated soles available from trekking stores can even be so small that they fit well in most concert shoes.

- There are also battery-heated socks which might fit better into most shoes.

- Wrist and ankle warmers, even hats.

- A cushion for cold chairs.

- Small electric blankets - there is almost always a possibility to connect it somewhere. Alternatively a hot water bottle.

- A thermos flask with a hot drink.

- Energy food.

It is also a good idea to have a room to get warm in in the breaks, with hot drinks, something the organiser of the orchestra should take care of.

Concert halls can be deceptively cold due to the air conditioning. In contrast to churches, concert halls have a strong tendency to be very dry, sucking all the humidity out of the strings and instruments. It even seems that strings stay more in tune in humid churches!

12 INTERVIEW WITH CELLIST CHRISTOPH HARER

Rachel: Cellists and violone players need to play so many more recitatives than other other string players, how do you practise them?

Christoph: Well, that depends on the type of recitative. If it is a secco recit with 'special effects' such as wild runs that need to illustrate something then I practise them in the usual manner. Otherwise it is often difficult if not impossible to practise recitatives alone at home. Least of all if they are in my own language. It gets more important if they are in a different language, especially one I don't speak well myself. I have to practise French ones very thoroughly so that I always know what is going on and my reflexes can take over. I need to prepare more for those.

R: You rely more on the texts in the recits?

C: Absolutely. What is really important is to know the text well so that I can react in the best way and even anticipate.

R: To follow the music rhetorically.

C: Exactly.

R: How did you learn to accompany recitatives?

C: As a schoolchild I sung along in many oratorios and loved listening to lots of recordings in advance. I soaked up this music. That helped a lot when I came to play my first oratorios as continuo cellist, especially in the recits. Playing recits was something I actually learned through lots of experience. I believe we need to gradually learn reflexes so as to notice what a singer wants to express at any given moment. And if he doesn't want to express anything, how we then might coax them into to adding some emotion!

R: You have a certain amount of influence.

C: Oh yes, definitely!

R: You have a conductor in front of you who wants to conduct the recitative; is that a problem for you, or can it be helpful?

C: That really depends on the situation and on the conductor. If the continuo group knows each other well and they are seated so that the performers can see each other well (e.g. the organist can see the cellist's bow), then conducting can be superfluous. There are conductors or choir directors whose conducting in the secco recitatives certainly is not helpful. They just want to conduct as a matter of principle, because it's 'their performance' ('how would it look if the conductor doesn't conduct?'). But really their conducting doesn't add anything of value, on the contrary it is more of a hindrance, because there is one movement to many and the instrumentalists don't necessarily know which impulse to react to. Follow the singer? Or only indirectly with the singer by reacting to the conductor and possibly being late? Or quite simply wrong. But enough of that: A really good conductor can of course be an enrichment! The question remains: is conducting necessary at this point in time? A very good conductor will add something of their own expression, which might be different to what I might do or spontaneously feel, but it would be something I could accept because it gives the recitative something special.

R: It is helpful in a tutti string recitative, an accompagnato, to have someone at the front.

C: Yes, especially because often the text isn't printed in the accompagnati. That can be especially helpful for the upper strings if there is something visual to follow.

R: When we look for a place for you to sit in the orchestra: is there a favourite place for the bass group to sit?

C: In the middle, please!

R: Do you have any preferences with which sections you have contact to? To each other?

C: I have the feeling that it does the whole orchestra good to hear lots of organ, or keyboard in general, as intonation has its fundaments in the keyboard. Besides, in baroque music the bass section has such a decisive roll, it is good if they can have as much direct contact to as many as possible and that is simply in the middle.

R: You are often put to one side. Do you notice a difference in the orchestra?

C: I do. I think the upper strings tend to do their own thing, that they feel like 'symphonic' upper strings. I often get the feeling that this right-hand side positioning of the bass group hasn't really been thought through. It probably comes more from a traditional orchestral set-up from a hundred or eighty years ago, so it doesn't tend to get questioned. We often get raised eye-brows if we suggest putting us in the centre, but I have rarely experienced that the suggestion wasn't successful. The only thing that needs to be decided is who sits to the left and who sits to the right of the bass section. Sometimes it can be difficult for the violins to be separated, especially if they have unisons and need to blend. Then it comes down to how well the orchestra is played in and they know each other. If both violin section leaders understand each other blindly then it doesn't matter if there are a couple of metres between them. We all need to make compromises sometimes!

R: What makes a good functioning bass section? Who should lead?

C: The answers can be quite different, depending on who you ask, a cellist or an organist, for example. Normally the continuo is led from the cello, if at all. Just because they seem to have the clearest movements, at least in comparison to a keyboard instrument or a bassoon (I'm probably going to get in trouble for this). Still, I don't believe that a continuo section is good when there is only a clear and strong leadership from the cello, that is definitively not enough. All players in the bass section need to fit in together, the cellists need to understand each other well and feel in a similar way. That actually goes for all the instruments in the bass group. The more harmonising together, the better one feels the music as a group, then the better it will function.

R: There are different styles of continuo leadership. With one you have to follow unquestioningly, with another the leaders are open to suggestions from the others. Have you had experiences like that?

C: Yes, definitely. Of course it depends very much on who else is playing and how much rehearsal time there is. Ideally, the basis would be that we appreciate each other musically and respect one another. If I notice while playing that there are interesting ideas from the others, or a suggestion is made in the rehearsal, then it's a good idea for me try it out and include it. First of all it can be an enrichment musically, and secondly it is important to keep everyone happy in the continuo section, not just the principal cello. That there isn't only one leader and all the others need to just function and follow. Or to hold themselves back musically for a homogenous interpretation. No musician can be satisfied if they have to do that for long. And I believe a musician who is unsatisfied with their job or their position cannot in the long run be a good musician. In that case, it is important not to lead autocratically, but to keep the hierarchies shallow. If at all necessary, but it probably wouldn't work without one.

R: Are you then the leader's reference person, so to speak? Is that your counterpart?

C: That is probably the case in a larger group. The smaller the ensemble, the more shallow and democratic it can all be, the leader can then speak to all of the continuo section. As in every section it would be ideal if everyone in the bass group could express themselves and there would be a joint musical understanding, so that it's not necessary to lead at all, just play together. However, it is practical in restricted rehearsal time when one person does the leading.

R: Talking about playing together: how does a bass section get the best sound?

C: Tuning well is a good start! On the one hand (because of our gut strings being so unreliable) always be awake and ask yourself: 'is the sound coming out of my instrument right now correctly in tune?', so that all who can really influence their intonation stay as aware as possible. On the other hand, everyone with a bow should bow as uniformly as possible, just as with the upper strings. Be very awake: how much bow are the others using? In general not too much pressure, at least on the cello, but with as open a sound as possible. If in doubt use more bow and less pressure. That helps for a more open bass sound which can mix better. It is always helpful hearing the organ, if there is one, as we lower strings can blend in well with that. That also makes a good section. It is difficult if we are too far from the organ, especially as a cellist, I find. There are other continuo players who would rather sit further away, e.g. lutenists, because they find their sound gets swallowed up. Or they don't hear themselves at all. I don't mind that, I like having a lot of organ.

R: What about the balance between violone and cello: how does the sound of the violone mix with that of the cello? Or is it the other way around?

C: It's probably important for the 8′ sound to be slightly stronger than the 16′, being the composed octave. Still, in a large line-up it is immensely important to have enough 16′, otherwise it can quickly sound too weak. I find it is extremely important that the cello and bass articulate as similarly as possible. The 16′ often needs to play shorter than the cello to be recognised as a unit. The resonance of the big instrument is longer, the sound of the violone lasts longer. On the one hand that can be wonderfully enveloping, on the other hand one could get the impression that the bass group doesn't articulate clearly. A lot of intuition is necessary as too much rough and short violone articulation can quickly become the opposite. It takes a lot of practise and knowing each other well. The amount of articulation varies of course from space to space, how much is needed varies depending on the different instruments.

R: Some churches are bass-heavy, some are upper string-heavy, or even oboe-heavy. Do you have any tips for that?

C: Even if a church is bass or oboe-heavy, they are certainly not bass-clarifying! My experience is: even if the bass is loud or quiet, it is never really easily understood. If in doubt, with an over-acoustic space, then articulate very clearly. Play extremely clearly, so that it seems almost absurd how short you play.

R: I find that we violins sometimes have to play with 'scratch articulation'. It sounds terrible directly at the ear, but further away it sounds perfectly articulated and round!

C: Absolutely, it can be frustrating when we have to perform in such a different way to how we feel the character should be.

R: Now for something different: when we play, it needs to be in tune! How do you think the strings tune best? I like it when the cello starts and the bass group tune on their own. I then take 'A' from the organ and compare it with you. There are many ways. What is your experience?

C: I think it is best when we try to reduce the 'Chinese whispers effect'. Something like this: the cellist takes his 'A' from the organ, then the concert master comes and takes the strings from the cello, goes to his section and passes it on. It could be that the 'A' in the back desks of the violins is a very different one to the one that originally came from the organ! Which is why it's good if the cellist can tune on his own with the organ and the concert master takes as much as possible directly from the organ. One possibility could be for the cellos and organ and leader pass on the open strings to the other string sections. That might save time, especially as we are always worried about missing the post-concert train because of our tuning orgies! When we take the notes from the organ, there seems to be a mysterious amount of room for interpretation. We can tune with approximations and it will still sound fine, so it really is a good idea to repeatedly check with each other.

R: It also depends where we stand around the organ, or how we bow our strings.

C: Especially when passing on to other people I ask my colleagues: 'Listen closely to my tuning! If you have a problem with it, please tell me!'. Rather than all sitting with badly tuned strings and not having said anything. It's so complex, no one is infallible.

R: And while playing, in a chord? Who is right? Is it always the keyboard?

C: Often, yes, which is why it is so important that the string basses sit near the organ. However it can be that if, for example, an organ 'Vallotti' has been tuned relatively equally, we strings can place the third somewhat nicer than the organ, yet it is still tolerable to the organ. As strings and bass strings we can tune with approximations that make keys nicer, without directly being out of tune with the organ. These are tiny nuances, but I find them necessary.

R: How do you take care of your strings in a concert? I know of fine-tuner pegs, but I don't think you use them?

C: I'm a bit of a purist there. I find it a not insubstantial appeal of our historical string playing to have to take particular care of the intonation, and that we practice getting in tune sounds from out of tune strings. I feel that is a large part of our role and a particularly athletic 'challenge'!

R: Then you play fewer open strings?

C: Yes, if needs be and they are already out of tune. Often the open strings are too low, then I can put a finger on them. Then I need be aware early on that at least with long notes or really obvious open strings that I need to be ready to put a finger on. If the strings go up then I need to go into a higher position, obviously. And as soon as the next opportunity comes discreetly turn the pegs and hope they don't make too much of a noise!

R: How would the best rehearsal schedule look for you? Do you ever get any breaks?

C: The best schedule from the point of the continuo section is a pessimistic one. One where there is just a little too much time for each piece so that there will definitely be a break. It is really hard work when a schedule is too tight. If certain details take too much time, the breaks get shortened or even cut because of this, then a day like that is just too much. That makes us just too knackered for the concert day. Not good for anyone. Rather an extra day of rehearsals!

R: Does it often happen that you rehearse into the breaks?

C: It usually starts with the recits, so it can happen that we are already behind when we start with the tutti, which is annoying for everyone. A good schedule always has a short break after 1½ hours.

R: And finally on a general matter: how do you interpret continuo playing?

C: What is my role in the continuo? Is it one where we organise the music, setting up a pattern over which others can move freely? Should I be a stable continuum, not distracted in tempo or metre and keep going quite calmly, never mind what caprioles the soloists or upper line are doing? Or is my job to be the perfect accompanist? To be amazingly flexible and follow the soloist with utmost awareness and read every wish from their violins or the singer's lips? The latter is in particular an ideal from the 19th century, prior that there are a number of sources saying that the continuo should remain stable. I believe however, that the truth is somewhere in the middle! It can't be that we compromise the soloist, just because they can't keep up, or they can't sing one bit fast enough or rush another. Showing up a soloist's weaknesses to the audience doesn't help anyone. I rather think it is a matter of balance, to be a stable frame on the one hand, but on the other hand empathising musically, moving a bit forward, a bit back. No reinforced concrete in the continuo, please.

R: Thank you for this interview!

C: You're welcome!

Christoph Harer, born in 1980 in Northeim, started learning piano, cello and organ at an early age. He studied the cello with Christine Aydintan as well as musicology, music education and German philology in Hanover. He studied baroque cello at the Royal Conservatoire in Stockholm with Mime Yamahiro-Brinkmann, following which he completed his education on this instrument with Viola de Hoog at the College of Arts in Bremen.

Presently living in East Frisia, he performs with various German baroque orchestras (Ensemble Schirokko Hamburg, la festa musicale, Das Kleine Konzert, Lautten Compagney, Musica Alta Ripa, Hannoversche Hofkapelle, Elbipolis Barockorchester, amongst others). As continuo cellist he has played for the North German Radio Choir, the Rheinische Kantorei (Hermann Max) as well as for the Kammerchor Stuttgart (Frieder Bernius). He has performed regularly at the International Handel Festival in Göttingen and at the Rheingau Music Festival. Concert tours have taken him to South East Asia, Mexico, Russia, Kazakhstan as well as frequently to the rest of Europe.

He is also active as a musicologist: in 2009 his book "Il Rosigniolo – Italiener in der hannoverschen Hofkapelle unter Herzog Johann Friedrich" was published by the Wehrhahn Verlag. His particular interests is in the research and transcription of German vocal music of the 17th century. He also works in early music for the Bärenreiter publishing house. In cooperation with the Herzog-August-Library in Wolfenbüttel he conceived and directed discussion concerts on literary themes in the baroque.

13 SOME FURTHER READING

Hans-Peter Schmitz – *Singen und Spielen* (Bärenreiter, 1958). A small but highly informative book concentrating on specific problems presented by musical lines, articulation, pitch etc. and how to counteract them.

Barry Green with W. Timothy Gallwey – *The Inner Game of Music* (PAN, 1986). A great book with many ideas on how to handle nerves!

Andrew Evans – *Secrets of Performing Confidence* (Methuen Drama; 2nd edition, December 5, 2013)

Susan Williams – *Quality Practice.* An excellent guide on practising! (www.susan-williams.com)

Ross W. Duffin – *How Equal Temperament Ruined Harmony* (Norton, 2007). A very good explanation of how temperaments work (amongst other things).

Ross W. Duffin – has also written an excellent article on why orchestras should use a simple 1/6 comma mean-tone: *Why I hate Vallotti (or is it Young?)*, https://castaculty.case.edu/ross-duffin/why-i-hate-vallotti-or-is-it-young-1-1/

Clive Brown – *String playing practises in the classical orchestra* (an article in the Basler Jahrbuch für Historische Musikpraxis XVII, Amadeus, 1993)

George Simon Löhlein – *Anweisung zum Violinspielen* (Leipzig & Züllichau, 1774). A historical treatise including how to play in an orchestra. Available on imslp.org.

Johann Friedrich Reichardt – *Über die Pflichten des Ripien-Violinisten* (Berlin and Leipzig, 1776). Yet another historical treatise including how to play in an orchestra. Available on imslp.org

14 ABOUT THE AUTHOR

Swedish born **Rachel Harris** began her baroque violin studies at the Welsh College of Music and Drama with Clare Salaman. After completing her studies with distinction she went on to a postgraduate at the Royal College of Music in London with Alison Bury. She was awarded the prestigious Countess of Munster and German Academic Exchange Service (DAAD) scholarships for her postgraduate studies in England and Germany. Her postgraduate studies were continued in Trossingen and Würzburg, Germany, where she concluded her soloist studies (Solistendiplom) with Gottfried von der Goltz, leader of the Freiburger Barockorchester. She also plays the viola, viola d'amore and the various instruments of the viola da gamba family (she has yet to try the violone...). In her free time she enjoys playing the horn.

She has performed (also as a soloist) in almost all parts of the world with Freiburg Baroque Orchestra, Balthasar-Neumann-Ensemble, Cantus Cölln, Lautten Compagney Berlin and La Banda Augsburg, with whom she has made a DVD recording of Vivaldi's Four Seasons. Other ensembles she has played with include the Orchestra of the Age of Enlightenment, Florilegium and St. James's Baroque, Deutsche Kammerphilharmonie Bremen and Deutsche Staatsphilharmonie Reinlandpfalz.

She has been a member of the English chamber music ensemble The Brook Street Band since 1997 and is the leader and director of Ensemble Schirokko Hamburg, which she formed in 2007. She has produced numerous CDs to critical acclaim with both ensembles.

In 2017 she released her solo CD »augustes auspices«, which is a complete recording of J.S. Bach's solo Sonatas and Partitas combined with J.P. von Westhoff's six Suites for solo violin. She can be heard regularly in concert with this programme.

As well as teaching privately, she is frequently invited to coach both baroque and modern orchestras. She is a guest coach and lecturer at the Hochschule für Musik und Theater Hamburg.

Furthermore there is a portrait of Rachel Harris in the book "Hier spielt die Musik! Tonangebende Frauen in der Klassikszene" ("This is where the music is! Leading women in the classical music scene") by Brigitte Beier and Karina Schmidt, AvivA Verlag, September 2011.

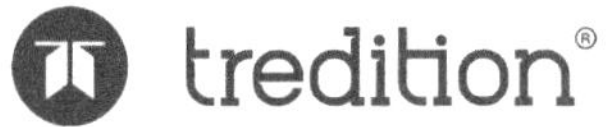